MODERN MYSTIC
Number Karma

GUIDE ...ND NUMEROLOGY NOTEBOOK

T0272201

A:ndrea Michelle
Art by Harper Rose

MODERN MYSTIC
Number
Karma

GUIDEBOOK AND NUMEROLOGY NOTEBOOK

Made with love by the team at

FiVE M.LE

Alex, Niki, Rocco, Graham, Jacqui, Claire, Amy & Lyndal

Five Mile,
the publishing division
of Regency Media
www.fivemile.com.au

First published 2022

Text copyright © A:ndrea Michelle, 2022

Restored Moon Symbol ©© A:ndrea Michelle, 2022

It is the author's experience with numerology that has led to the content
of this book. It is an amalgamation of the author's interpretation of varying
strands of information from both ancient and contemporary sources.

Illustrations copyright © Harper Rose Tattoo, 2022

Printed in China 5 4 3 2 1

CONTENTS

Introduction to numerology   **7**

     Welcome   9–10

     Mystic words   12–13

     A brief history of numerology   15–16

     Co-creating with karma   17

Essence numbers   **19**

     Your essence number   21

     How to find your essence number   22–23

Essence number meanings   **25–40**

     Action and inaction   40–41

Pathway numbers   **43–44**

     Examples of Pythagorean pathways   45–46

     Chaldean pathways   46–49

     Updated Chaldean pathway numbers   50–56

     Chaldean pathways 23–52   57–62

     Numbers, language and trauma   62–63

Peak pyramids and your power years   **65**

     What are peak pyramids?   66–68

     What are power years?   69–70

     Personal year numbers   70–71

The power of your name   **73**

     Unlocking the power of your name   74

     Finding your freewill number   75

     The three number planes   76–77

     Balancing your number karma   77–79

     Understanding your name's numerological frequency   79–81

     Balancing your karma with loved ones   81–83

     To the Modern Mystic community   84

Reference section   **87–90**

Bios   **93**

     About the author   94

     About the illustrator   95

INTRODUCTION

TO

NUMEROLOGY

Welcome

Whenever -ology is found at the end of a word, it translates as 'the study of'. *Number Karma* is therefore your personal guide to a world of numerology. Within these pages, you will learn how to consciously direct your numbers to act in their highest potential for you.

The numerical valuing of letters, names, dates, musical notes, colours, planets, places and things describes patterns of energy that manifest within our lives and environments. They have effect upon us whether we are conscious of them or not. The great gift that you have, modern mystic, is your openness to understanding more about these patterns and how you can work as a harmonious co-creator with them.

We applaud you for choosing to bring more joy and balance into your life, and also thank you for the service this plays in helping to make our world a better place.

Do not underestimate the power of even the smallest positive change that you make. Each little shift contributes more significantly than what many have, to now, allowed themselves to imagine.

As with so much of our conditioned thinking and language, evolution is needed, which is why you have been magnetised towards this *Number Karma* book. You are a vital link within a growing unified global community of people waking up and becoming evolutionary agents. Though not everyone is going to identify with the tag of mystic, anyone committed to helping see a better world for all is in their own way a modern mystic. That is, they are:

- Seeking to find a greater sense of unity
- Seeking to feel more peaceful inside
- Remembering that they are enough always, in every way

Let us share with you how else *Number Karma* will be helping to bring greater balance and harmony into your life.

In this book you will learn about:

YOUR ESSENCE NUMBER

Calculate and then activate the untapped gifts and resources that are held within your innate power number.

PATHWAY NUMBERS

Become adept in the steps that will prepare you to optimally express the full potency of essence numbers.

PEAK PYRAMIDS AND POWER YEARS

Calculate when your four power years occur so as you can prepare yourself to get the most out of these significant, peak-energy times.

RENEGOTIATING DESTINY

See how your number frequency signature can change by shortening a longer name, changing your name or how it is spelled, adopting a nickname or pseudonym, or exchanging your surname through marriage.

BALANCING YOUR NUMBERS

Optimise your fullest potential through rebalancing any excesses, deficiencies and/or missing links in your numbers.

COMPLETING YOUR NUMBER KARMA

Understand how you, your friends and family can help one another in the actualisation or completion of 'number karma'. This section includes learning how to check the numerological compatibility of partners.

Live and let live. Judge no other, and always, be open to grow and change.

Shine brightly.

Love, the Modern Mystic team.

Mystic words

Below is a list of words that you will come across in this book.

CHALDEAN NUMBER SYSTEM

The Chaldean number system is a numerological way to interpret numbers based on sound frequencies.

ESSENCE NUMBER

An essence number is a single digit number resulting from adding the numbers of your birth date together. Through learning about both the gifts and shadows of this number, you are gifted with insights into your innate nature.

FREEWILL NUMBER

This number is also known as your 'destiny' or 'expression' number. It is derived from and related to your given birth name as well as any other names by which you are known. It differs from your essence number in that you can change your name, and so, have full freewill power to change your destiny.

KARMA

The interpretation of karma that is used in this book is sourced from the Sanskrit root of the word: karma = action.

NUMEROLOGY

Numerology is the study of numbers. Through this study of numbers, insight is gained. This insight can then be utilised to bring greater peace, balance and empowerment into your life, and so, into the life of our world.

PATHWAY NUMBERS

A pathway number is the final composite number before it is reduced to a single digit. These numbers gift a richer understanding of what needs to be mastered before the essence number may truly shine.

PEAK PYRAMID

One of four activating numbers. It is calculated from your birth date.

PEAK YEARS

Your age when the peak power periods (pyramids) occur.

PERSONAL YEAR NUMBER

This is found from adding the day and month of your birth to the current year. Knowing and keeping track of which year number you are in is of great advantage to your life.

PYTHAGOREAN NUMBER SYSTEM

The Pythagorean number system is a numerological way to interpret numbers using the Latin (Roman) alphabet.

MYSTIC,
POSITIVELY ACTIVATE YOUR NUMBER FREQUENCIES AND RECLAIM YOUR POWER AS A CO-CREATOR

A brief history of numerology

There are various systems of numerology. The two that this book will cover are the Pythagorean and the Chaldean. The major difference between these systems is the way sound-values are designated.

The Pythagorean number system

You may be familiar with Pythagoras' name. Ancient Greece, triangles ... well, you can now add 'personae within the lineage of numerology' to your brain's CV file on him. It is a simple but highly informative system, with an inbuilt bias towards the West.

In the Pythagorean system, the value of each letter is based upon the sequence of the Latin (Roman) alphabet: A=1, B=2, C=3 ... I=9, etc. This then repeats up to Z=8 as can be seen below:

The Pythagorean Number Values

1	2	3	4	5	6	7	8	9
A	B	C	D	E	F	G	H	I
J	K	L	M	N	O	P	Q	R
S	T	U	V	W	X	Y	Z	

The Chaldean number system

The Chaldean number system is the older system of numerology. In the ancient times of Sumeria and Babylon, the people were connected to the natural world and listened respectfully to its cycles, including those of the moon. (Chaldean carries within it the meaning 'moon-worshipper'.)

During their age, temples were built in alignment with the seven known planets. Colours, metals and numbers were attributed to each. The Chaldeans lived near the banks of the Euphrates River in Mesopotamia, our present-day Middle East. The peoples of this time are currently credited with the creation of both modern astrology and number lore.

The Chaldean number system varies from the Pythagorean system in that it assigns value based on sound or frequency. Theirs is not an arbitrary, linear methodology. It is founded upon the lineage of cuneiform, where, by way of example, the pictogram of a bird is used to relay a sense of freedom:

By considering the Chaldean calculation and interpretation of your numbers, you will be able to bring into your awareness additional dimensions of meaning that are not represented within the Pythagorean system. Both are helpful and valid in guiding you on your mystic path.

The Chaldean Sound Values

1	2	3	4	5	6	7	8
A	B	C	D	E	U	O	F
I	K	G	M	H	V	Z	P
J	R	L	T	N	W		
Q		S		X			
Y							

You will notice that the Chaldeans did not assign any letter or sound to the number 9. The tablets left by them indicate that this was because the number 9 was regarded as being highly sacred and connected to the divine. Later, you will learn that their tablets also only recorded pathway numbers up to the number 52. We will be giving you more information as to why they chose to do this when we get to the pathway section.

For now, maybe drink some water and nestle in to learn a little more about you becoming a number alchemist.

Co-creating with karma

Karma has different meanings to different people — this is as it is meant to be. Whatever your personal belief, or disbelief, for the time we spend together within this volume in our Modern Mystic series, the interpretation of karma that will be used is sourced from the Sanskrit root of the word:

KARMA = ACTION

So, this is a book about ways you can learn how to consciously direct your numbers to **act** in their highest potential for you.

Around the time when Babylon became the largest city in its world, there was a book written named the *Sefer Yetzirah*. It contained instructions, mystic paths of wisdom about how to become a co-creator of your own life. The text also nominated that our spiritual realm is shaped via the sound of the letters that make up our names and other words. This ancient book recorded the knowledge that we are articulating our world into being.

When you speak the pet-name of your lover, best friend, sibling, grandparent, or one of the various names of your beloved pet, you are participating in an alchemical act. You are creating a living presence of a certain vibration that has a real-world effect. You will be learning later on exactly how you are providing a unique and irreplaceable role in altering and improving the reality of those whom you love most in this world.

But first, let's discover your most potent numerological tool, your essence number.

ESSENCE NUMBERS

WHAT OUR WORLD
NEEDS IS FOR
PEOPLE TO
FOCUS ON WHAT
EMPOWERS,
RATHER THAN
ON WHAT
DEPLETES

Your essence number

In this section, we are going to show you how to unlock and activate what is, in numerological circles, generally called your 'ruling number'. However, mainly because we are not fans of old-world hierarchy, we will be referring to the power that is revealed from inside your birth date as your 'essence number'. Finding your essence number is calculated by adding up the three key components of your birth date: the day, month and year.

Why your birth date?

Your name can change. The day that you were born does not change. This is the case even if you transition your body's expression. Your essence never alters. Therefore, your essence number reveals something which is intrinsic, essential and belonging completely naturally to you. It is your sweet-spot number, and one that is very important for you to become not only super-familiar with, but to also keep activated so that its full potential may blaze gloriously within your life and all who are touched by your life.

In your journey of becoming your most luminous mystic self, your essence number is going to become one of your superpowers. It will be a tool, a peace-weapon, that you will be able to start using straight away in the process of re-envisioning your life.

How to find your essence number

Finding your essence number is done by simply adding your birth date numbers together to get one, single digit number.

The equation to follow is:

DAY + MONTH + YEAR

It is important that you don't collapse any numbers, especially the year. For example, if you were born in 2010, be careful not to just use 10 instead of 2010. the 2 is an important part of the equation.

When doing your equations, be sure that you have reduced your day, month and year to single digits before adding them together.

An example of finding your essence number is below:

- You were born on the auspicious eve of 01/01/2001.
- To get your essence number, simply add the three components together:

$$(0+1)+(0+1)+(2+0+0+1)=5$$

Meaning, your essence number is 5.

Here's another example, and it's important you follow this part before trying your own:

- Let's say that you were born at high noon on 17/10/1998.
- If we follow the same method as we used for 01/01/2001, we get:

$$(1+7) + (1+0) + (1+9+9+8)=36$$
$$3+6=9$$

This method is incorrect. Please in no way feel confused by this. Just remember that whether it is a name, a date or a thing, you always need to work out each component of whatever you are considering down to its single digit as step one, then once you've done this, add these together as step two.

The correct way to find this essence number is:

DAY + MONTH + YEAR

(1+7)+(1+0)+(1+9+9+8)

(8)+(1)+(27 which is 2+7=9)

(8)+(1)+(9)=18

1+8=9

The end result is the same, 9. Your essence doesn't change, but the pathways vary. In the first example that is incorrect, the pathway or composite number is 36, however, in the above example, it is 18. You will soon understand completely why this is relevant in relationship to providing you with your correct pathway information. As too, why it is a necessary step for when you do the calculations for your peak pyramid periods.

We will see you when you return from your *Numerology Notebook* (the essence number section on pages 2–5) with your essence number.

Now that you have unlocked and so liberated one of your biggest resources of power, you may like to calculate the essence numbers for your family and friends too. If this is the case, you will begin to learn about an aspect of your basic numerological compatibility with others.

Please use your *Numerology Notebook* on pages 2–5 to write out:

- The qualities of your essence number.
- The shadow tendencies to patiently overcome.
- The qualities for you to joyously and expansively cultivate, and more importantly, tend to as living presences in your life.

Maybe there are many positive qualities of your essence number already expressing themselves through you and how you are in this world. If this is the case, hooray for you. The unlocking part may not be needed so much as the continued activation of this essence throughout the rest of your life.

ESSENCE NUMBER MEANINGS

The meaning of numbers 0 through to 9

Below is one unified reference point for the combined essence of the qualities of each number from 0–9 as offered by the Chaldean and Pythagorean number lineages.

Where we have found conflict or discrepancy in perception, we have focussed upon the points of unity and greatest empowerment for you.

We have also included an image that you may like to reflect upon as a non-finite symbol for each essence number.

It is important to note that 'yang', referenced as an attribute of 1, is not connected in any way to what has been traditionally accepted as masculine or male. For our dawning new age, we are reconnecting this energy with the natural action of fire and air. Both have a tendency to rise up in the direction of the sky.

Likewise, 'yin' as an attribute of 2 is not connected to what has been traditionally accepted as feminine or female. In this context, we are reconnecting it with the natural action of water and earth, both of these having a tendency to move towards or be within our precious, wise Earth.

We trust that you will enjoy this new phase in your modern mystic journey.

1

Qualities and tendencies:

- Visionary leadership
- Individuality
- Co-creative independence
- Initiating and/or pioneering action
- Work/life/play infused by spiritual purpose
- The essence of yang

Shadow tendencies to patiently overcome:

- Arrogance
- Self-righteousness
- Intolerance
- Unhealthy pride
- Everything that ends in -ism such as sexism, ageism, racism, nationalism
- Those false 'need' feelings to be someone who is important, famous, universally liked

Qualities to joyously and expansively cultivate:

- Inclusiveness
- Clear focus
- The confidence to lead
- True humility
- The fire to take action

In a personal year 1:

- Make a new start
- Dare to pioneer

- Take on a leadership role
- Free yourself from co-dependent relationships
- Align more closely with your spiritual, mystic purpose

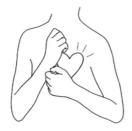

2

Qualities and tendencies:

- Intuition
- Cooperation
- Discernment
- Compassion
- Balanced relationships
- Receptivity
- Intelligent love
- Peace-making
- Meditation
- Wise Earth guardianship
- The essence of yin

Shadow tendencies to patiently overcome:

- Fear
- Over-sensitivity
- Passivity that becomes procrastination or laziness
- Over-consumption (such as food, shopping, sex, alcohol, drugs)
- Co-dependent relationships
- Doubting or not honouring intuitive impressions

Qualities to joyously and expansively cultivate:

- Trusting and acting on your intuition

- Feeling okay being on your own or enjoying quiet time alone
- Staying centred
- Practically caring for the Earth
- The peace within yourself to live and let live

In a personal year 2:

- Re-centre from the dynamic energies of the previous year 1
- Reconnect or establish a time for consciously breathing each day
- Spend more time with the natural world
- Ensure you are Earthing/Grounding yourself regularly
- Tune in more to your intuitive knowing
- Reassess all your relationships through a lens of harmony and balance
- Recalibrate if you have been over-giving
- If you are feeling depleted or resentful, re-establish healthy boundaries
- Enjoy cooperating with others

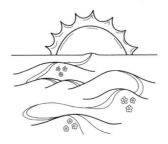

3

Qualities and tendencies:

- Expand your mind and keep it clear
- Connect with how you best learn so that learning is a joy
- Travel
- Accurately verify 'facts'
- Access higher imagination and be creative
- Believe in luck

- Be open to miracles
- Communicate succinctly

Shadow tendencies to patiently overcome:

- Losing clarity via exhaustion and/or substance abuse/ use
- Over-busyness
- Preoccupation with money
- Stagnation of your mind
- Allowing anger or other habits to overshadow reason
- Allowing your mind to be too easily distracted or swayed by illusions
- Arrogance from feeling mentally superior
- Reinforcing a less than ideal reality by repeating any mantra to do with you having a poor memory
- Blocking your creative expression

Qualities to joyously and expansively cultivate:

- Clarity
- Creativity
- Quietness in your mind
- Enjoying learning
- Sharing only truth

In a personal year 3:

- Study something new
- Travel
- Communicate
- Learn more about meditation and/or mindfulness practices so that your mind can optimally function
- Stop or reduce any habits you may have developed that leave your mind dull or scattered
- Be creative, artistic, imaginative

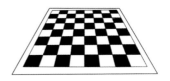

4

Qualities and tendencies:

- Structured work and discipline
- Bringing order from chaos
- Facing and overcoming inner turmoil
- Being practical, steadfast, stable, steady, organised
- Securing your financial realm
- Consolidating
- Expressing beauty
- Consciously working with colour(s)

Shadow tendencies to patiently overcome:

- Being over-materialistic
- Getting stuck
- Losing work/life balance due to overworking
- Being disorganised
- Messy
- Being financially irresponsible or frivolous
- Rejecting or blocking colour and beauty from being in your life
- In-fighting within yourself
- Being in states of perpetual conflict and criticism within yoursef and also with and about others

Qualities to joyously and expansively cultivate:

- Positive self-discipline
- Enjoying work
- Harmonious order in your personal environment
- Staying grounded
- Art
- Relationship with colours
- Inner sense of serenity and beauty

In a personal year 4:

- Consolidate your life by making your structures stronger or more coherent
- Recalibrate your work/life balance
- Tidy
- Resolve conflict(s) in yourself and/or with others
- Create beauty
- Explore colours more

5

Qualities and tendencies:

- Freedom
- The green that is reflected from the vibrant, natural world
- Allowing the vital energy of nature to heal and reopen your heart
- Laser-focus to pursue truth
- Invention
- Knowledge
- Discovery
- Adventure
- Exploration
- Investigation
- Careful research
- Refining and simultaneously expanding expertise
- Honouring sensitivity
- Grounding the voices of nature in art

Shadow tendencies to patiently overcome:

- Wanting fame or accolades to substantiate worth

- Losing your 'Centre'
- Desiring endless freedom but reciprocating nothing of value back into life
- Too narrow a focus
- Not living inclusively
- Arrogance of scientific rationalism
- Overlooking the essence that lives through the form-world

Qualities to joyously and expansively cultivate:

- Enjoying the journey of discovery
- Being nourished through contact with the natural world
- Clear discernment

In a personal year 5:

- Write two lists: one for what gives you a sense of freedom and one for what gives you a sense of limitation or constriction. Can you take fresh eyes on any of the limitations and see them instead as paths to greater freedom? If not, use this year to rebalance this
- Clean up your knowledge on whatever interests you most
- Spend more time with healthy plants
- Open to the possibility that current scientific models do not hold every answer
- Meditate upon this statement from *A Course in Miracles*: *Nothing real can be threatened. Nothing unreal exists.*

6

Qualities and tendencies:

- Devotion
- Visionary ideals/fanatical idealism
- Global family/personal family
- Commitment
- Loyalty
- Intelligent love
- Positive thinking/negative thinking
- Overcoming extremes and extremism
- Seeing that you, unlike the untamed ego, are not addicted to psycho-dramas, alienation and all manifestations of cruelty
- Creativity from the inspired mind
- Actualised self-responsibility
- Correct detachment

Shadow tendencies to patiently overcome:

- Misplaced devotion and misguided fundamentalism
- Subconscious addiction to mental negativity
- Limiting your sense of family to your immediate circle of friends and relatives
- Ignoring useful impressions that are coming in to positively guide you towards a freer and more purposeful life
- The habitual tendency to be on the defensive

Qualities to joyously and expansively cultivate:

- Intelligent love

In a personal year 6:

- Begin to make small but consistent steps away from fanaticism and misplaced devotion. If you are unsure if your current belief systems are healthy expressions of the '6' energy, simply ensure that you are harming no other
- Reprioritise your primary sense of loyalty to building greater peace inside your own head
- Listen to the subtle impressions you are receiving and allow them to become grounded in the world as healing forms of art and beauty

7

Qualities and tendencies:

- Spiritual wisdom
- Living ritual and ceremonial magic
- Introspection and deep reflection
- The need for positive solitude
- Inner and outer world balance
- Self-discipline
- Self-discipline directed towards diet and exercise
- Purification
- Living with the expectation of vital health
- Studying the literature of sacred mystery, mystic and occult lore
- Psychic awareness
- Teaching

Shadow tendencies to patiently overcome:

- Wasting your vital energies on things that hold no true meaning
- Being swayed away from your intuitive knowing by the voices of others
- Making good plans in your head but not acting on these plans
- Rigidity

Qualities to joyously and expansively cultivate:

- Clear discernment
- Surrender to the ever-deeper layers of the divine in you
- Trusting in your ability to create and maintain vital health
- Sharing true beauty with the world

In a personal year 7:

- In consultation with a health professional if this is indicated, dedicate at least half a day each week to herbal tea or water fasting. If this is not safe for you, experiment with fresh organic vegetable juices or, when it is in season, eat nothing but fresh watermelon for the first half of a day once a week to help re-alkalise your body. Start each day by drinking warm water with a squeeze of either fresh lemon, lime or grapefruit juice
- Familiarise yourself with Jerry Tennant's work on cell voltage and pH levels
- Take fresh eyes on your omega 3 and pure water intake
- Reprioritise your schedule so that you have some designated space just for you
- Read some spiritual literature
- Purify your tendencies to critically judge yourself and others
- Teach

8

Qualities and tendencies:

- 8 is an infinity loop. Two complete beings coming together in their totality
- A Möbius strip
- The essence of 'one life' with no boundaries
- Bringing or manifesting spirit into matter
- Actualising or grounding projects that are in alignment with spiritual purpose
- Transformational and transmutational healing
- Being active in the broader world
- Self-confidence
- Revelation of karma
- Surrender to acceptance in divine justice
- Infinite possibilities
- Reclaiming the multidimensionality of your true self

Shadow tendencies to patiently overcome:

- All belief in destructive divisiveness

Qualities to joyously and expansively cultivate:

- If you are oriented towards a traditional faith, feel its presence in all areas of your life
- If you feel repulsion towards all organised faiths, stay open, away from hate, and enjoy meeting the infinite facets of your mystic self

In a personal year 8:

- If you have been in alignment with your spiritual purpose, your mystic self, this is the harvest time for whatever you started in your personal year 1

- A power year. Reward, recognition, material/financial/physical plane success
- A year you can actualise your self-healing from ailments
- If life circumstances have meant you have not been able to live these past 7 years in alignment with your mystic self, go gently. There is a new cycle that will begin for you in two years' time. Prepare yourself for this

9

Qualities and tendencies:

- Humanitarian service that extends equally into practical care for all life, including animals, plants and the natural world
- Visionary projects
- Compassion, but not in relationship to the origin of this word 'to suffer with', rather, compassion in the context of 'love in action'
- Being motivated to do things for the greater good
- Benevolence
- Healthy expressions of selflessness
- Growth from a broadened perspective
- Unwavering integrity
- Inspiring others to realign with their own heart-truth
- Endings and completions
- Releasing the past
- Renewing or releasing existing relationships
- Balancing karma

Shadow tendencies to patiently overcome:

- Destructive forms of both selfishness and selflessness (driven by unintegrated forces along the martyr-victim axis)

- Inability or reluctance to release what is no longer serving your highest good
- Hating, condemning or wishing ill on any life form that does not subscribe to your personal interpretation of reality

Qualities to joyously and expansively cultivate:

- Unshakable integrity
- Tolerance and acceptance of difference
- Non-attachment
- Joyously being in roles of service

In a personal year 9:

- Complete what you began in your previous personal year 1
- Have the courage to prune, to let go, to move on
- Volunteer some of your time or donate some of your resources to the betterment of life outside your immediate family unit
- Prepare the seeds you wish to sow in your coming new cycle

0

Qualities and tendencies:

- Innate unique gifts
- Peace with and expressions of interconnectedness
- 0 is an amplifier: increasing voltage, frequency, power
- Enhances the positive potentials of other number(s)

- Later you will learn about anaretic degrees. The 'o' also acts in an enhancing, activating capacity, bringing out the most potent expression of any other number energy it touches

Shadow tendencies to patiently overcome:

- Blocking or hiding your magnificence

Qualities to joyously and expansively cultivate:

- Increasing awareness of the interconnectedness of everything
- Living life and generously sharing with the world your full potential
- Being the sky

Action and inaction

Just as there is a certain potential within water sitting in a bottle in your bag, and a different potential of this same water once you have drunk it, your numbers also express varying potentials just waiting to be activated.

Say, for example, you have just worked out that your essence number is '7'. You have read the text, taken in what the qualities and shadow qualities are about, but then, in two months' time, instead of using your freewill to express some life-affirming action of your essence 7, you choose instead a shadow tendency.

Or, you opt for non life-affirming inaction.

At this point there is an addition to the definition of karma. The expanded version is:

> Your number karma
> asks to be understood
> within the context that
> non-action is an action too

Drinking water once, or for a short period of time, is not going to satisfy your body's needs for the rest of your life. This is the same as you reading about your essence 7, but then not continuing to consciously tend to its clearest expression.

Inaction can also express in positive ways. Some examples of this for a person with an essence number 4 are:

EXAMPLE 1

- You are talking with a friend and the conversation turns towards another person who is not there. You then find that you are about to participate with your friend in a session of verbal character assassination of this other person.
- You could use this opportunity to change your number karma for the better, by not joining in with this non-productive conflict and negative criticism.

EXAMPLE 2

- You are feeling flat and heavy.
- You start online shopping even though you are already in debt and there is no room in your wardrobe.
- You see some shoes at ridiculously low prices. It is one of the simplest things that you can do to help yourself and this world's environment: take the very potent path of inaction and start your rehab away from excessive materialism by not purchasing the shoes.

PATHWAY NUMBERS

Pathway numbers

Whilst the goal is to reduce composite numbers down to a single number, there is useful and important medicine on the path to that single number.

Hierarchal structures have been useful learning tools for previous ages, but they are not a part of our now dawning Aquarian age. With this adjustment in mind, you will be able to better understand that there is no 'better or worse' in relationship to whether your essence number has arrived into your world with or without a pathway number.

Let us show you what we mean by a pathway number using our previous examples:

EXAMPLE 1:

Birth date: 01/ 01/2001
Essence number: (0+1) + (0+1) + (2+0+0+1)=5

In this example, there is no pathway number for this person to move through and in turn learn in order to embody the optimal expression of their essence number 5.

EXAMPLE 2:

Birth date: 17/10/1998
Essence number: (1+7) + (1+0) + (1+9+9+8)=18
1+8=9

This person has the pathway number of 18. From the Pythagorean system, this person is being guided to unlock and activate the energies of 1 and 8 so the fullest potential of their essence number 9 may shine. An example of this may be to trust in their vision, be a leader and pioneer a new innovation (1). In doing this, money will manifest (8). They can then use their wealth to support worthy humanitarian causes and so, improve conditions for humanity as a whole (9); or to put it simply:

Innovate (1) + make money (8) = help others (9)

Examples of Pythagorean pathways

Here are some examples of pathway numbers from the Pythagorean system. You can see that we have very basically selected and combined key qualities from the single numbers 0-9.

$$34 = 3 \text{ \& } 4 \text{ (7)}$$

Clear thinking, creativity and openness to the reality of common miracles (3) alongside disciplined work expressing beauty (4) will help to bring vital health, spiritual wisdom and a balanced inner life (7).

$$12 = 1 \text{ \& } 2 \text{ (3)}$$

Leadership, action and initiative (1) along with intuitive stillness and cooperation (2) will open and expand the mind, allowing it to express higher forms of creativity (3).

$$44 = 4 \text{ \& } 4 \text{ (8)}$$

NOTE: Disregard everything you may read elsewhere about 4 and 8 being hard karmic numbers. This thought-field belongs back with the previous ages.

Careful, patient, steadfast work and discipline, bringing order from chaos that expresses beauty (4 & 4) will enable you to manifest spiritual vision into matter. By doing this, financial reward and recognition from the broader world will come (8).

$$20 = 2 \text{ \& } 0 \text{ (2)}$$

For this pathway, it is important that you listen more to your intuitive voice (2). If an impression flashes through your mind to take an umbrella, take it. Even if you look outside and see a blue sky. Use time to slow down and be still. Seek harmony, cooperation and balance in your relationships (2). There are incredible possibilities that live in you. Infinite and multidimensional, you are already everything (0). Becoming the peace that is within silence allows you to step into your role of compassionate Earth-healer and guardian (2).

10 = 1 & 0 (1)

Single pointed focus with the willingness to not just talk but take decisive and just action (1), coupled with a life-long commitment to use some space every week to look at the sky and remember that you are that (0) will allow you to emerge and decisively act as a true pioneering leader (1).

There is space on pages 6–9 of your *Numerology Notebook* to discover yours and others' pathway number(s). We trust these examples will help you understand your own pathway numbers, and so, help you to become more deeply connected with your true heart and unique purpose in this world.

PATHWAY NUMBERS AND ASTROLOGY

Not having a pathway number is similar to having an anaretic degree (the finalising 29th degree in each zodiacal sign) in astrology. The word anaretic is seeded from a Greek word meaning destroyer. Think destroyer in terms of eliminating all else but the pure expression.

Though texts from our previous ages have tended to place the focus of their interpretation on the potential shadow expressions of these degrees, we opt to perceive both them, and essence numbers without pathways, as very singular and potent expressions of energy.

Chaldean pathways

The Chaldean system has its own unique and mystical associations for pathway numbers up to and including number 52.

Let us use the example:

Birth date: 17/10/1998
Essence number: $(1+7) + (1+0) + (1+9+9+8)=18$ (9)

From the Chaldean perspective, the pathway advice for this person is significantly different to that of a Pythagorean pathway. If you happen to feel drawn to research other sources, you will soon learn that Chaldean pathway number interpretations can vary from text to text, with some translations transgressing quite significantly into the shadow-lands of fear and disempowerment.

18 happens to be one of the bleaker offerings. Brace yourself. We have compiled a number of different versions, a little abbreviated, but carrying the general meaning:

- This number is difficult to relay via symbolism: a ray moon dripping blood; a wolf and hungry dog drinking the falling blood; a crab hastening to join the feast
- The pathway of 18 is one of materialism destroying spirit and nature
- Pathway 18 influences a person to quarrel bitterly, especially within one's family
- Social upheavals, revolutions, wars
- Making profits from wars
- Be warned of treachery and deception by others
- Be guarded
- Act with caution and circumspection
- In calculating dates in advance, avoid 18
- Danger from tempests, water, fire and explosions

How are you feeling? Uplifted and inspired?

Our sense is no, this amalgam interpretation for pathway 18 has neither uplifted nor inspired. The complete opposite of what we are wishing for you. Though it may feel like a little detour at this point, we are going to give a little backstory for two of the pathway numbers, 18 and 26. We are doing this so that you may more fully understand the power of thought, suggestion and intention whilst on your mystic pathway.

The numbers 18 and 26

First, we will look a little more closely at one aspect of the dated archetypal pattern ascribed to the Chaldean pathway number 18: The Moon.

In Western Astrology, amongst other attributes, the moon is associated with the mother figure and the sun with the father figure. Up until now, the moon in this system has been depicted by the crescent phase of the moon. A partial representation of a greater whole.

There is a reference made in the Bible about Eve being made from the rib of Adam (Genesis, 2:22). A partial representation of a greater whole. Though Eve is currently accepted within this tradition as being the first woman, you may like to read up on Lilith (Black Moon) who, it can be interpreted, is referenced earlier in Genesis, 1:27, as being made as a complete equal with Adam.

It is pretty clear to people on this planet that most of the governing systems that were seeded within previous ages are broken. What people may not be so aware about, is how the symbols and language we use reflect and perpetuate these broken and disempowering institutions.

We move together as one people through into Earth's new age. Your third-eye opens, mystic, your heart senses what is true and empowering. Within the spirit of equal opportunity for all, the time of 'the mother', the 'deep feminine' being partially represented, in every context, is over. Following soon within the 'Updated Chaldean pathway numbers', you will find our revised offering for pathway 18.

But first, to reinforce how important it is for you to understand how programmed language can negatively recreate your world, here is another paraphrased traditionally accepted version for the pathway number 26:

- This number comes with the gravest warnings
- Ruin brought about via partnerships, unions, bad advice and ill-fated speculation
- It foreshadows disasters brought about by association with others
- If it is calculated as your pathway number, be warned, question every step you take

We feel a little deflated even typing up the translation for this Chaldean pathway number. It expresses so little light, and so, has no resonance with a mystic's path.

The old world, run by disempowering or fear-based directives, is dead. Not only dead, but also being revealed as being unsound. This is highlighted by the pathway number for the word 'starlight', a word that describes the light coming from the centre of our solar system and one which allows all life to thrive in this world:

$$S\text{-}T\text{-}A\text{-}R\text{-}L\text{-}I\text{-}G\text{-}H\text{-}T$$
$$3+4+1+2+3+1+3+5+4=26$$

Very different from the traditional description of pathway number 26.

Maths is a symbolic language of numbers. Pythagoras showed how we can positively enhance wellbeing through harmonic frequencies. Numbers are symbols and symbols can heal. It is from this lineage that we return the moon's symbol to wholeness:

No longer partially represented.

The Moon restored as a full symbol embodying and respecting the changing faces.

Reframing Chaldean pathways

There is a fundamental inconsistency between fear-based directives and those which are seeded with intentions to assist people in reaching their highest potentials.

It is understood by less spiritually awakened people that a way to maintain control over another person, or other people, is to keep that person, or the critical mass of people, in fear and feeling divided. This division is destructive enough when it is seeded between person and person—as we see in cases such as conditioned racial hatred. But the more insidious divisive forces are the ones that leave a person, or people, in their own unique ways, fragmented, scared or uncertain inside.

It is for reasons such as these above that we have reformulated some of the Chaldean composite or pathway numbers from their former shadow-lands. We also voted around our round table to leave an abbreviated summary of the traditionally accepted pathway interpretations. These are marked for you as being from the previous age. They are included mainly so you can feel the difference inside you when you read them.

The first interpretation, we hope, will give you a sense of hope. Whilst some of the traditional interpretations may generate a sense of looming unease, possibly even dread. Not exactly helpful feelings in any age.

Updated Chaldean pathway numbers

The numbers 10 through to 21 embody similar qualities and mirror the guidance shared through the cards 10 through to 21 in the Tarot's Major Arcana. If you have our Modern Mystic set, 'True Tarot', you may be familiar with the Tarot cards shown in this section.

10

Tarot card: Wheel of Fortune

CARD 10

Wheel of Fortune

- Breathe to find your heart's voice, your calm and centred place within. It is from this space that you can steer and navigate your life with the greatest ease and joy
- Nourish your inner altar
- Take time to ground and learn to trust what is felt but not always seen

From the previous age:
- One's name will be known for good or evil
- A fortunate number in the sense that one's plans are likely to be carried out

11

Tarot card: Strength

CARD 11

Strength

- If you opt to use your freewill to stay immersed in the surface of material possessions, empty titles of elitism, compulsive sex devoid of love and artificial appearances, there can be, over time, a dulling of your ability to make contact with true joy
- The world of forms is there to be enjoyed, but this pathway reminds you that the wisdom way is to keep this in balance with spirit and nature

From the previous age:
- Symbols: a clenched hand; a lion muzzled
- An ominous number
- Warnings of hidden dangers, difficulties, trials and treachery from others

12

CARD 12

The Hanged Man

Tarot card: The Hanged Man

- Look at anything that feels harsh in your world from a new perspective
- If you can, literally hang upside down. Or look at yourself in a spoon
- This pathway number is asking for you to start to interpret your reality in a different, more positive way
- Realign with your inner light and silently state from this place exactly what you need. The resources that you need will come once you believe that you are truly worthy of receiving them
- If you are feeling as though you are trapped and have no choice, know now inside your bones that it is this belief that is your real trap

From the previous age:
- Suffering and anxiety
- Symbols: a sacrifice; a victim
- The foreshadow of one being sacrificed for the plans or intrigues of others

13

CARD 13

Death

Tarot card: Death

- The only constant thing is change
- When a purpose has been fulfilled, a new sense of purpose comes to fill the space
- Trust to let go, something better always comes

From the previous age:
- Symbols: a skeleton; a grim reaper
- Dominion and power
- Up-heaval and destruction
- Warning of the unknown or unexpected

14

CARD 14

Temperance

Tarot card: Temperance

- You are far more than what you think you see in the mirror
- Aim today to gently merge and therefore create greater

harmony between your heart and your mind, your body and your inner essence

From the previous age:
- Movement
- Danger from natural forces—water, air, earth, fire
- Fortunate for money and changes in business, but with a constant risk of damage from the arrogance of others
- Warning to act with caution and prudence
- A 'command number'

15

Tarot card: The Devil

The Devil

- Symbol: an inverted five-pointed star
- When spirit is re-prioritised, the natural world will regenerate
- When spiritual lore is shunned, and the base desires for ever more power, empty lust and greed dominate, nature and earth life suffer
- If this is the pathway number, tune into an eight-year orbital cycle of Venus and as you do, allow yourself to absorb into your psyche the higher metaphysical teachings from this planet

From the previous age:
- If associated with a fortunate single number, it can be lucky and powerful
- If associated with 4 or 8, 'black-magic' may be evoked to gain desires
- Lower occultism. Associated with eloquence, gifts of music, art, drama and personal magnetism
- Favourable indications for receiving resources from others

16

Tarot card: The Tower

The Tower

- If this is the pathway number, it is important that you begin to honour the quiet messages that your heart has been giving you. Although these intuitions may not feel like they suit your reality to hear, you need to make real world changes based upon them now
- Even if change means that everything that you know and trust might come tumbling, crashing down,

remember: a phoenix always rises up gloriously from every pile of ashes
- If you are already adept, or as you become more adept at responding fearlessly to your mystic self, you will find that things will stop falling down around you. This is when you will be ready to embody the higher aspects of 7

From the previous age:
- Symbols: a tower struck by lightning; a shattered citadel
- Warning of strange fatality, accidents, defeat
- Plan and act carefully

17

Tarot card: The Star

The Star

- **Even when the moon is dark, stars are always there as points of light. Remember that you are made of star-stuff. It is no made-up thing—stars that go supernova are what create the elements that make up your physical body. From your smallest building blocks, you are already essentially a self-luminous star**
- **This pathway is an activation for you to shine more brightly than you have ever shone before**
- **Understand that as you allow your true light to be seen, it serves as a navigation point for others to move from their dark-nights**

From the previous age:
- Symbols: eight-pointed Star of Venus; star of the Magi
- The spirit rises above the trials and difficulties of life and career
- A highly spiritual number
- A number of immortality—name lives on
- A fortunate number in relation to future events, provided it is not associated with the single numbers of 4 and 8

18

Tarot card: The Moon

The Moon

- **Reclaim your unity. Calmly voice 'no' to all that diminishes and/or only partially represents your true worth**
- **Identify and transform all shadow tendencies that obstruct you from being a clear vessel for wisdom**

- Just as the moon reflects, learn to lovingly self-reflect
- The veils of illusion part as you name and release non-productive attachments from your past and, in doing so, unite more closely with your mystic essence
- If guides present themselves to assist you, listen attentively to the voice of your heart. Always ensure any guide you choose to follow is a Being of Light
- The medicine of a lunar bird, the owl, may assist you in hearing your heart's voice, by reminding you to reflect more closely on any shadow-self deception if a guide happens upon your way as a 'wolf in sheep's clothing'

From the previous age:
- Symbols: a ray moon dripping blood; a wolf and hungry dog drinking the falling blood; a crab hastening to join the feast
- Materialism destroying spirit and nature
- Bitter quarrels with family
- Social upheavals
- Wars and profiting from wars
- Danger from tempests, water, fire, explosions
- Treachery and deception from others
- Be guarded
- Avoid 18 when planning dates

19

Tarot card: The Sun

CARD 19

The Sun

- Just like the sun in our sky, live from your Centre and cast no shadow
- Release all impulses to justify or explain who/what/how/where/why you are; let go of seeking approval from others
- Shine without hesitancy or apology

From the previous age:
- Symbols: the sun; the Prince of Heaven
- Promises for happiness, success, fortune, esteem and honour
- Favourable for future events

20

Tarot card: Judgment

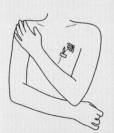

CARD 20

Judgment

- Listen and watch for the little signs
- If you begin to notice that you are habitually needing

to clear excess mucous from your nose, consider investigating potential dietary triggers and/or your spinal alignment
- If there are angry people around you, look more closely at unresolved issues of anger in you
- Make positive adjustments
- Orientate your focus away from empty materialism towards spirit and nature
- Wake up

From the previous age:
- Symbols: a trumpet sounding; people awakening from tombs with their hands clasped in prayer
- The call to action, cause, duty, purpose
- Not a material number so unlikely to achieve worldly success
- Delays and hindrances to one's plans which can only be conquered through the development of the spiritual nature

21

CARD 21

The World

Tarot card: The World

- Completing spiritually-oriented purpose
- The gathering of the seed essences learned through this completion to take into the next octave of your mystic path

From the previous age:
- Symbols: the universe; the crown of the Magi
- Advancement, honours, success
- Victory after long initiation and tests of determination
- Fortunate in any connection to future events

22

- There can be false glamour around 'master numbers' such as 11 and 22
- All numbers will assist you towards greater mastery when expressed in life-affirming ways
- To live harmoniously with others, you must first learn to live from a place of harmony within yourself
- Listen to your intuition and cultivate the strength to stay connected with your own intuitive knowing
- This is especially important for you to do when the forces and voices around you become domineering with authoritative declarations which may not ring as true

inside your heart-mind
- Over the doorway leading to the Delphic Oracle in ancient Greece were words instructing each seeker to 'know thyself', 'to thine own self be true'

From the previous age:
- Symbols: a good man living in a fool's paradise; a good man offering no defence against the attack of a ferocious tiger; a man with a knapsack full of arrows on his back; a man blinded by the folly of others
- Illusions and delusions
- Dreamer of dreams
- False judgment owing to bad influence from others
- Warning to take extra care if this number is linked with future events

Do not feel confined by negative pathway meanings

It is important to remember to accept only the information that can genuinely assist you in manifesting what is life-affirming; that which can help you change your life and this planet for the better.

If you have the Modern Mystic set, 'Finding Your Mystic Self', you will already have this card:

There are no limits other than those limits
that you allow to be placed on you.
There are no limits.

Bringing this frequency of thought deeply into all of your cells is one of the fastest and most powerful ways to effect positive change and healing not only for you, but for all in this beautiful world. Make it a new practice.

Simply replace whatever feels fear-based or divisive in your thinking with anything that is more positively uplifting and harms no other life.

Chaldean pathways 23–52

Up until this point, we have offered a reformulated interpretation of the Chaldean pathway numbers, with the traditional lineage of translation noted as being from the previous age.

Reality appears to shift only when a critical mass of our world's population freely agrees to accept a change, so as a new mystic, we encourage you to write your own interpretation of the pathway numbers of 23–52 and beyond.

Then, if you feel drawn, please share your insights with other modern mystics in your life and/or the broader mystic community.

Until then, here are the abbreviated traditional interpretations:

23

- Symbol: royal star of the lion
- Success and help from superiors
- Protection from those in high places
- A fortunate 'command' number

24

- Promises assistance from those of rank and position
- Gain through love and associations with the opposite sex
- Favourable when calculated in relationship to future events

25

- Strength gained through experience
- Benefits obtained through observing people and things
- Not considered 'lucky', as success only comes through strife and trials in earlier life
- Favourable in regard to the future

26

- Gravest warnings for the future
- Foreshadowing of disaster brought about by association with others
- Ruin by bad speculations, partnerships, unions and bad advice
- If calculated in connection with future events, be careful

27

- Symbol: the sceptre
- Promise of authority, power and command
- Rewards from the productive intellect
- Creative faculties sow good seeds that produce abundant harvests
- A 'command number'
- Do not be swayed by others, rather, ensure you carry out your own ideas and plans
- Fortunate number in any connection with future events

28

- Great promise full of possibilities
- However, there is the likelihood that all gained will be taken away unless careful provisioning is made for the future
- Loss through trusting others
- Opposition and competition in trade
- Danger of loss through law
- The likelihood of having to begin life's road over and over again

29

- Uncertainties, treachery and deception by others
- Foreshadowing of trials, tribulations and unexpected dangers
- Unreliable friends
- Grief and deception from members of the opposite sex
- Very grave warnings if it comes out in connection with future events

30

- Thoughtful deduction and retrospection
- Mental superiority over one's fellows, though this superiority belongs completely to the mental plane
- Likelihood of putting all material things to the side
- Neither fortunate nor unfortunate, the manifested reality for this pathway depends upon one's mental attitude
- Accordingly, there is potential for either great power, or indifference about power

31

- Kin to pathway 30, except there is greater self-contraction, loneliness and isolation from one's fellows
- Not a fortunate pathway from a worldly or material perspective

32

- Magical power kin to the single 5 and the 'command numbers' 14, 23 and 27
- Associated with nations and combinations of people
- Fortunate if personal judgment and opinions are defended
- If this is not the case, likelihood of things being wrecked by the stubbornness and foolishness of others
- Favourable if calculated in connection with future events

33

- Same meaning as the number 24

34

- Same meaning as the number 25

35

- Same meaning as the number 26

36

- Same meaning as the number 27

37

- Good and fortunate friendships
- Good for partnerships of all kinds
- Fortunate if calculated in connection with future events

38

- Same meaning as the number 29

39

- Same meaning as the number 30

40

- Same meaning as the number 31

41

- Same meaning as the number 32

42

- Same meaning as the number 24

43

- Unfortunate
- Revolution, upheaval, strife, failure and forces that block and prevent evolution
- Unfortunate in calculation relating to future events

44

- Same meaning as the number 26

45

- Same meaning as the number 27

46

- Same meaning as the number 37

47

- Same meaning as the number 29

48

- Same meaning as the number 30

49

- Same meaning as the number 31

50

- Same meaning as the number 32

51

- Unique and powerful potency
- The nature of the warrior
- Promise of sudden advancement in all undertakings
- Especially favourable for those in the military and naval life
- Blessed for leaders in any cause
- Threats by enemies
- Danger

52

- Same meaning as the number 43

Why do Chaldeans finish at 52?

Earlier we mentioned that we would give you some more information about why the Chaldeans chose to stop at pathway 52.

It appears that this choice was linked to their belief in the sacredness of the numbers 9, 5 (one of their 'command numbers') and 7 (the number of known planets at that time).

$$9 \times 5 = 45$$
$$45 + 7 = 52$$

You may now like to calculate yours and your loved ones' Chaldean pathway numbers in your *Numerology Notebook* on pages 10–13.

Numbers, language and trauma

It is such a tender point in our world circa 2022. Millions, perhaps billions of people are living under varying degrees of trauma, including transgenerational or intergenerational trauma. For those of you who are unfamiliar with this term, it has to do with the collective pain that is passed from unhealed ancestral wounding through into new generations.

If this topic raises any issues for you, we encourage you to please contact support networks such as 1800RESPECT (1800 737 732), a 24-hour national sexual assault, family and domestic violence counselling line for any Australian who has experienced, or is at risk of, family and domestic violence and/or sexual assault. If you are in immediate danger, call 000 for police and ambulance help.

In his book, *The Biology of Belief*, Bruce Lipton taught us how much more potent and distorting this force of pain is when compared to pure genetic inheritance.

The intention behind this Modern Mystic series is to facilitate healing. We understand that each person who is given the space and love to holistically heal contributes immeasurably towards collective healing.

For this to occur on the scale that is required we need, at the minimum:

- Multiple sacred spaces for deep listening
- Practical resources
- A reorientation towards inclusiveness
- The spiritual will of leaders to transcend old-world red tape
- A reconfiguration of symbols and language

Any displayed attitude or behaviour that society deems as 'bad' or 'wrong', is perpetrated out of a place of unhealed pain.

It is trauma, or unhealed pain and confusion, that seeds all shadow-land thought, feeling and action in people.

This is one of the main reasons why evolved mystics teach love, tolerance, inclusive sharing, forgiveness, kindness and compassion as the true paths in this Earth-life. The uglier, crueler, more divisive, hating and exclusionary the thought, feeling or action of another person or body of people, the greater the need is for us to listen with fresh ears to that pain.

It is to do with this re-imagining that we are inviting you, dear mystics, to join together and reweave the pathways. It is in our unified collective power to dream a more loving world into being.

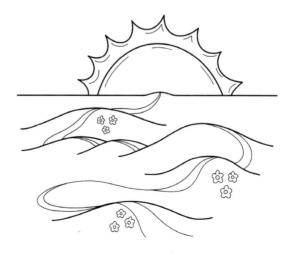

PEAK PYRAMIDS AND YOUR POWER YEARS

What are peak pyramids?

A peak pyramid is a way to find the essence numbers for your personal 'power years'.

How to create your peak pyramids

Below are step-by-step instructions on how to create your peak pyramids using the birth date 17/10/1998. You may recognise a lot of these calculations from when you worked out your essence number.

To help make it super easy for you, we have summarised this section on page 89. You will find room for your calculations in your *Numerology Notebook* on pages 14–17.

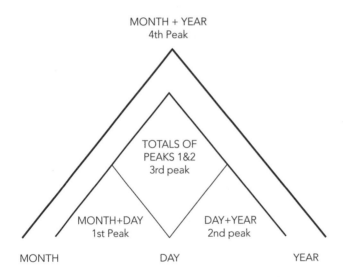

STEP 1: LEFT PYRAMID FOUNDATION

The first step in creating the foundation of your pyramid is to reduce your MONTH to a single digit.

Example:
October (10) 1+0=1

STEP 2: MIDDLE PYRAMID FOUNDATION

The second step in creating the foundation of your pyramid is to reduce your DAY to a single digit.

Example:
17th day of the month: 1+7=8

STEP 3: RIGHT PYRAMID FOUNDATION

The third step in creating the foundation of your pyramid is to reduce your YEAR to a single digit.

Example:
1998 = 1+9+9+8=27. 2+7=9

STEP 4: 1st PEAK

Next, add the totals of the MONTH and DAY. This will reveal the essence number for your 1st peak pyramid power year.

Example:
1 (October) + 8 (17th day)=9

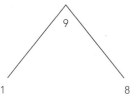

STEP 5: 2nd PEAK

Now add the totals of the DAY and YEAR from the middle and right side of your foundation. This will reveal the essence number for your 2nd peak pyramid power year.

Example:
8 (17th day) + 9 (1998)= 17. 1+7=8

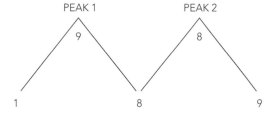

STEP 6: 3rd PEAK

Add the totals of the 1st and 2nd peaks together. This will reveal the essence number for your 3rd peak pyramid power year.

Example:
9 (1st peak) + 8 (2nd peak)= 17. 1+7=8

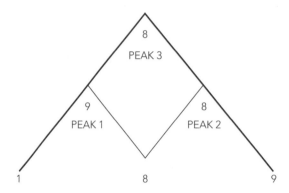

STEP 7: 4th PEAK

Finally, create the 4th peak by adding the two corners from the base of the pyramid by adding the MONTH + YEAR.

Example:
1 (October) + 9 (Year)=10. 1+0=1

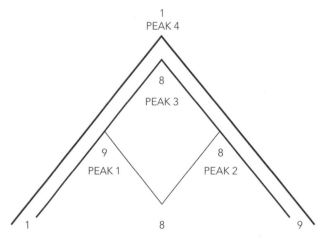

Whatever the 4th peak is for you will be a guiding and informing number for the rest of your life. Please, go now and have fun dicovering your four peak pyramids.

What are power years?

'Power years' are unique to each person. You can think of them as years when the essence number really wakes up and becomes a positive living presence in your life. To prepare for your power years, it is a wisdom-way to lovingly and systematically clear the shadow tendencies of your coming peak pyramid number before the year starts. This then will open the clearest portal for that essence number to express through you into our world.

From the pyramid that we just created, the peak pyramid essence numbers for the birth date 17/10/1998 are:

9 (peak 1)
8 (peak 2)
8 (peak 3)
1 (peak 4)

Calculating your power years

Just as the Chaldeans had reverence for the number 9, the builders of the pyramids had a kinship with the number 36. This is one of the main reasons that it is used as the base number from which you deduct your personal essence number to reveal the age you will be when your first power year occurs.

POWER YEAR 1=36 – (minus) YOUR ESSENCE NUMBER

Using the birth date example of 17/10/1998, the essence number that we established previously is 9. Therefore, the age at which the first peak pyramid occurs for this person is:

36 minus 9=27 years

Then, each of the remaining three peak pyramids occur at nine-year intervals.

So, for the person born on 17/10/1998:

Age 27 – peak 1 (Essence Number 9)
Age 36 – peak 2 (Essence Number 8)
Age 45 – peak 3 (Essence Number 8)
Age 54 onwards – peak 4 (Essence Number 1)

This is why Elders are such treasures for this world. They are residing in their constant, peak-power expression.

Using this calculation method, please find space to add in the four ages next to your pyramids on pages 14–17 of your *Numerology Notebook*.

Personal year numbers

As with most things, there is debate on the correct methodology when it comes to the calculation of your personal year number. Some people do it from the start of the year, others do it from their birthday. From our observations, tailoring specifically to your birth date gifts greater accuracy. But you can feel this out for yourself.

For sensitive people the changing of energies, such as a Solar Return chart in astrology, is felt about three months leading up to your birthday. You may experience the same feeling with the change in your personal year numbers too.

Of all the computations, this is probably the easiest one, and can be very helpful to keep track of throughout your life:

PERSONAL YEAR NUMBER=BIRTH DAY+MONTH+CURRENT YEAR

Remember: you must first condense the DAY, MONTH and YEAR numbers into single digits before adding them together.

For example, if we use the birth date of 01/01/2001 and the year this book was published, 2022:

day (1) + month (1) + current year (2022: 2+0+2+2=6)
1+1+6=8

This person's personal year number for 2022 is 8.

Using the birth date from our previous example, 17/10/1998, this person's personal year number is 6.

(1+7) + (1+0) + (2+0+2+2)
8+1+6=15. 1+5=6

Please turn now to the space we have left for you on pages 18–19 of your *Numerology Notebook*. Then once you have found your personal year number, simply refer back to the 'Essence number meanings' section.

The guide that you have on pages 27–40 is non-finite. We welcome you to share new ideas you have about your personal year numbers, and anything else that may assist in uplifting consciousness, with your mystic community.

THE POWER OF YOUR NAME

Unlocking the power of your name

The United Nations Convention on the Rights of the Child stipulates that all new babies are to be legally registered. Once this is done, there is a name on a form that carries with it a certain frequency.

This name may or may not end up having a 'living presence' in your life. It depends upon whether or not your full title is frequently spoken out loud, and whether the spelling gets changed, as can be the case when longer names are shortened.

Many of us have a much grander title than the one that is used in our day to day lives. Have you noticed how some people develop a whole entourage of alternative names for the people or animals who they love most? Maybe you are one of these people? Shortening a longer name, changing your name or how a name or names are spelled, adopting a nickname or pseudonym and exchanging your surname through marriage are all examples of how your freewill can come in and alter number and energy frequency signatures of your name.

Until the point when you legally have your name changed in the official government database, the number value of the title that you were given at birth, including the exact spelling, becomes what is customarily accepted in numerological circles as your destiny or expression number. However, there is something about the word destiny that feels a little fixed. We therefore will be referring to the number signature of your birth name as your 'freewill number'.

For you to be able to understand how you may benefit via the modification of your registered birth name, the following section will provide you with the information you need.

Finding your freewill number

As we are considering two systems of numerology, you will soon learn that your freewill number may end up having two different frequency signatures, as well as two different, but mutually supporting pathways.

To show you the method for finding your freewill number, we will use the name Modern Mystic.

MODERN MYSTIC

M O D E R N   M Y S T I C
4+6+4+5+9+5=33   4+7+1+2+9+3=26

(3 + 3) + (2 + 6)
6 + 8 = 14
1 + 4 = 5

The Pythagorean freewill number for Modern Mystic is 5, with the pathway numbers of 1 and 4. You can use the 'Essence number meanings' section to understand the numbers within the pathway and this freewill number.

For reference, here is the freewill number using the Chaldean system:

M O D E R N   M Y S T I C
4+7+4+5+2+5=27   4+1+3+4+1+3=43

(2 + 7) + (4 + 3)
9 + 7 = 16
1 + 6 = 7

The Chaldean freewill number for Modern Mystic is 7, with the pathway number of 16.

Please go now and joyfully unlock the power of your name using pages 20–23 in your *Numerology Notebook*. Once you have found your freewill number, we will then be able to give you the pointers and resources to convert this information into healing and greater empowerment for you.

The three number planes

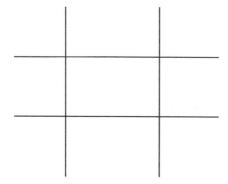

You may recognise the image above as a naughts and crosses game grid ready to be played. For numerologists, it also doubles as an important tool used to help people see and understand their constitutional make-up.

Due to the omission of any letter designated to 9 in the Chaldean system, for this following section, please only refer to the Pythagorean number values when doing the calculations for you and your loved ones. We have left room for this on pages 24–25 of your *Numerology Notebook*. There is also a summary on page 90.

It is the grouping of letters on each of the three horizontal planes that we will be exploring.

3 — C L U	6 — F O X	9 — I R
2 — B K T	5 — E N W	8 — H Q Z
1 — A J S	4 — D M V	7 — G P Y

The three main number planes are:

3–6–9 top row: the mental plane—mind, reason, intellect, memory

2–5–8 middle row: the emotional plane—feelings

1–4–7 bottom row: the physical plane—practical doing

The mystical, spiritual, soul, intuitive plane is of course present in all three. Just as each of the three planes are co-mingled with one another. An example to help you better understand this interdependence is if certain nutrients are missed on the physical plane of diet, the mental plane of mind and memory is more likely to suffer from diminished acuity.

Balancing your number karma

It is from this point that you can really begin understanding your numerological constitution, and so, start making helpful remedies and/or modifications.

In your *Numerology Notebook*, please turn to the section titled 'The three planes' on pages 24–25. There you will find a series of number grids. The first thing that you need to learn is if your birth date has at least one number frequency on each of the three planes.

We will show you some examples of what we mean:

EXAMPLE 1: BIRTH DATE 17/10/1998

		9 9
		8
1 1 1		7

Considering the three major planes, a person born on the 17/10/1998 has at least one frequency point represented upon each level, plus the extra gifts of 0.

EXAMPLE 2: BIRTH DATE 01/01/2001

```
        |        |
        |        |
  _____|_____|_____
        |        |
   2    |        |
  _____|_____|_____
        |        |
  1 1 1 |        |
        |        |
```

A person born on 01/01/2001 does not have any number frequency on the top row. This could mean a range of things: there may be difficulties with memory and/or focussing the mind; or maybe, the person is gifted intellectually or a conceptual genius, rarely understood by other minds.

A parent or guardian discovering this about their child would be advised to lovingly observe, and if it became indicated, intervene by way of making a modification within the freewill number, the child's name.

If this child had not yet been named, a balancing effect could be gifted by selecting a name, or reconfiguring the spelling of a preselected name, that included some of the letters with the values of 3, 6 and/or 9 which are absent in the birth date. There are many gifts from 0.

Changing your name as an adult

If you are already 28 and have just found out you have an absent plane, look, think and feel first if any change is necessary.

If you sense yes, look at how you can help rebalance the energies by making a change to the living presence of your name—that is, the name that you hear spoken out loud the most frequently.

If you feel uncertain, or consider it too big of an ask for people to start calling you by a different name, fret not, there are always other options that you can explore.

Another approach is to leave your name as is, but turn your will towards perfecting, to the best of your ability, one of the three absent numbers from the row. It may be the number that seems most foreign to you, or the one that feels most resonant.

You equally may decide to bring all three of the numbers into a greater living presence in your life.

For the person in our example born on 01/01/2001, the '3' could be selected and developed through doing cryptic crossword puzzles. Another mode of development could be becoming an exchange student for a year. Or the 3, 6 and 9 could be evolved through the study of an endangered, indigenous language.

Understanding your name's numerological frequency

Now that you know which of the numbers in the three planes are represented by your birth date, the next phase in the process of balancing your number karma is to use your *Numerology Notebook* (pages 24–25) to explore your name's numerological frequency.

Here is an example using the name Modern Mystic:

3 — C	6 — O	9 — I R
2 — T	5 — E N	
1 — S	4 — D M M	7 — Y

In this example, you may notice that you have filled in lots on certain rows, and little on others. This is all valuable data. For what we are looking for are not only natural strengths, but also excesses, absences and deficiencies. Once we know these, we can then go a little deeper into the process of rebalancing and optimising your number karma to its fullest potential.

How to work with number deficiencies

If you have discovered that you are missing certain numbers, or that you have an empty plane, the following section has some suggestions that may be able to help you. Working with your deficiences can help you to 'own' or integrate into yourself a clearer expression of a number or plane, simply because you are bringing greater mindfulness towards it. It can also bring added benefits.

For example, a person without any 2s, 5s or 8s may like to adapt these meal suggestions:

- Eat five almonds
- Place two organic cardamom pods, slightly crushed, into your coffee
- Slice two rings of fresh ginger and place them on top of one another. Cut these into four, giving you a total of eight pieces of ginger to put into your cup of tea (you could also read up on the health benefits of cardamom and ginger)

Your options are infinite. Just like you.

Too many of the same number

An excessive representation of a number can represent an imbalance just as equally as an absence or deficiency.

Consider a person born on the 22/02/2021. Not only are there five number 2s, the essence number is also 2 (1+1). The pathway of double 1 along with the 1 from 2021 hold the potential to bring into this person's life the impetus for dynamic action. But other than this, mindfulness would need to be kept so as the shadow energy of essence number

2 does not adversely shape the life expression. Balance could be gifted via the name. Alternatively, this person may be an advanced spirit who has incarnated with a very specific purpose related to the frequency of 2.

THERE'S NOTHING WRONG WITH
AN ABSENT NUMBER PLANE

It is so important that you do not feel defective in any way if you have an empty plane or any other absent numbers. You could very well learn over time that it is a secret peace-weapon of exceptional value. Trust that all an empty plane or number frequency does is highlight a need to bring closer awareness towards that number or plane. Once your mindfulness has been directed towards it, you can joyfully actualise the qualities it represents into your life, and so, the life of our world. In doing this, you rebalance your number karma. So dear modern mystic, feel good about you—expanded and optimistic.

Balancing your karma with loved ones

Another approach to help balance your numbers is to do a number study of those people who are closest to you. By familiarising yourself with their numerological profiles, you will inevitably find someone else who has the number frequency/ies that you are missing. Equally as helpful, you don't even need to personally know the person, or place. Just allow your mystic self to guide you towards what you need for your optimal flourishing.

An example of this for a person with an absent bottom row (no 1s, 4s or 7s) is to entrain with the immense capacity for 'practical doing' within the beautiful woman who helped edit this book, Amy (A=1, M=4, Y=7). A look into interconnectedness, quantum entanglement and mirror neurons will help you to better understand, and so activate, this powerful, natural capacity within you.

On the next page you will learn another technique for helping rebalance your number karma with others. It involves carefully moving through each letter of each name, one at a time, checking the Pythagorean chart and systematically placing a mark in accordance with the absence or presence of a number frequency in each name.

For this example, we will use one of your alter-ego identities, Modern Mystic, and a spiritual teacher who you may find to be of great assistance on your path, Eckhart Tolle.

We have only added the detail on this chart to make sure it's as easy as possible for you to follow and so replicate your own.

PYTHAGOREAN NUMBER VALUES

1	2	3	4	5	6	7	8	9
A	B	C	D	E	F	G	H	I
J	K	L	M	N	O	P	Q	R
S	T	U	V	W	X	Y	Z	

	MODERN MYSTIC	TOTAL		ECKHART TOLLE	TOTAL
1		(s in Mystic)	1	1		(a in Eckhart)	1
2		(t in Mystic)	1	2	||| (k, t in Eckhart and Tolle)	3
3		(c in Mystic)	1	3	||| (c, l in Eckhart and Tolle)	3
4	||| (m,d, m in Modern and Mystic)	3	4		0
5	|| (e and n in Modern)	2	5		(e in Eckhart)	1
6		(o in Modern)	1	6		0
7		(y in Mystic)	1	7		0
8		0	8		(h in Eckhart)	1
9	|| (r in Modern and i in Mystic)	2	9		(r in Eckhart)	1

This computation shows that through Modern Mystic's association with Eckhart, via listening to and reading his Work and allowing what is between the words he shares to enter into the deepest places inside, there is the potential for the missing '8' to become actualised, or completed. As far as Modern Mystic helping Eckhart, he is a spirit already woken. And so, his missing 4, 6 and 7 are within a state of grace and balance as him.

We trust that you are understanding better all the time, how we are each providing a unique and irreplaceable role in altering and improving reality for one another.

Equipped with the full name of any other person, place or thing that you are wishing to learn more about, please turn to pages 26–31 of your *Numerology Notebook* and continue with the rebalancing of your number karma.

This simple, highly informative technique will not only allow you to better understand how your friends and family can help you balance and complete your number karma (and vice versa), you will also be able to check the numerological compatibility with your partner, or potential partners in your future.

Examples of balancing karma

Before departing from your lovely company, here are a few other examples of how you can balance your number karma:

1. You have no 9s but your partner does. Your partner volunteers half of each second Saturday preparing meals for disadvantaged people (essence number 9=humanitarian service work). To balance your number karma, you start going with him.
2. You have no 7s, but the garden and soft green grass does (the letter G=7). Learn about Earthing/Grounding and how you need to be making bare skin contact with the natural world in order to establish and maintain vital health (7).
3. You have either none or low representations of 3s, 6s and 9s in your name and birth date. You are always misplacing your keys and forgetting things. 'Library' has four energies living in it from this plane (the letters L, I, R, R). Help your mind, visit the library.
4. You have no 2s but your grandmother has buckets of 2s. You ask her to teach you how to knit and how to meditate. You then add this reminder into your phone or year planner: *Breathe slowly. It's ok to be still.*

FURTHER READING

If you are particularly interested in this section, there are many resources you can explore that go into greater detail about the meaning of other planes or 'arrows' that are not just considered along the horizontal planes, but vertical and diagonal as well.

To the Modern Mystic community

As our world reconfigures from COVID's varied traumas, a critical mass number of people have reappreciated the incredibly important role actual real-life contact with other people is. Many have rediscovered that it is one of the greatest gifts that there is.

As part of our world healing, you are now an activated mystical agent with potent healing knowledge. We trust this knowledge will not only help you with feelings of anxiety from not understanding why you haven't been feeling enough (the endless 'enoughs'), but that you will also feel naturally and abundantly motivated to keep this healing knowledge alive in you for the rest of your time here on this planet.

To help yourself with this, go and enter some appointments into your phone, making sure your message alert is on. Or if you like paper, enter some appointments with yourself for two months from now, then six months, and so on. If you have just found you have no active 7s, your message to yourself might be '7' or 7?. If you don't have any 8s or 1s, your message might be 8? 1?. Also make a note towards the end of each year to make new appointments. Maybe you can experiment setting these for the spring and autumn equinox each year, the days when light and night are in balance.

Your capacity to self-heal is unlimited.

REFERENCE SECTION

Pythagorean number values

1	2	3	4	5	6	7	8	9
A	B	C	D	E	F	G	H	I
J	K	L	M	N	O	P	Q	R
S	T	U	V	W	X	Y	Z	

Chaldean sound values

1	2	3	4	5	6	7	8
A	B	C	D	E	U	O	F
I	K	G	M	H	V	Z	P
J	R	L	T	N	W		
Q		S		X			
Y							

Finding your essence number

Your essence number is a single digit number resulting from adding the numbers of your birth date together.

Equation:

DAY+MONTH+YEAR

Example: Birth date 17/10/1998

(1+7) + (1+0) + (1+9+9+8)

8+1+27=9 + (2+7)

9+9=18

1+8=9

Finding your pathway number

Your pathway number is the number BEFORE you reach your singular, essence number.

Example: Birth date 17/10/1998

Pathway number:
(1+7) + (1+0) + (1+9+9+8)=18

Essence number:
(1+8)=9

Note: some people may not have a pathway number.

Creating your peak pyramids

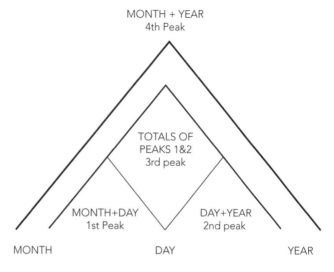

MONTH + YEAR
4th Peak

TOTALS OF
PEAKS 1&2
3rd peak

MONTH+DAY
1st Peak

DAY+YEAR
2nd peak

MONTH   DAY   YEAR

Add the MONTH + the DAY =1st peak pyramid

Add the DAY + the YEAR =2nd peak pyramid

Add the TOTALS of PYRAMIDS 1 and 2=3rd peak pyramid

Add MONTH + YEAR =4th peak pyramid

Finding your power years

Deduct your essence number from the designated number of 36.
This will give you your age for power year 1. Then move in 9 year
increments up to your power year 4.

POWER YEAR 1 = 36 – (minus) your essence number
POWER YEAR 2 = Your age for power year 1+9 years
POWER YEAR 3 = Your age for power year 2+9 years
POWER YEAR 4 = Your age for power year 3+9 years

Finding your personal year number

YEAR NUMBER = BIRTH DATE + MONTH + CURRENT YEAR

Remember: you must first condense the DAY, MONTH and YEAR
numbers into single digits before adding them together.

Finding your freewill number

The number value of the title that you were given at birth, including the exact spelling, becomes your freewill number. Calculate using Chaldean and Pythagorean values.

The three number planes

Planes and their meanings:
3–6–9 top row: the mental plane—mind, reason, intellect, memory
2–5–8 middle row: the emotional plane—feelings
1–4–7 bottom row: the physical plane—practical doing

3 — C L U	**6** — F O X	**9** — I R
2 — B K T	**5** — E N W	**8** — H Q Z
1 — A J S	**4** — D M V	**7** — G P Y

Balancing your karma

Balance your karma by checking your name with other people, places or things. Follow the Pythagorean number system for this computation (example below).

	MODERN MYSTIC	TOTAL		ECKHART TOLLE	TOTAL
1	| (s in Mystic)	1	1	| (a in Eckhart)	1
2	| (t in Mystic)	1	2	||| (k, t in Eckhart and Tolle)	3
3	| (c in Mystic)	1	3	||| (c, l in Eckhart and Tolle)	3
4	||| (m,d, m in Modern and Mystic)	3	4		0
5	|| (e and n in Modern)	2	5	| (e in Eckhart)	1
6	| (o in Modern)	1	6		0
7	| (y in Mystic)	1	7		0
8		0	8	| (h in Eckhart)	1
9	|| (r in Modern and i in Mystic)	2	9	| (r in Eckhart)	1

BIOS

About the Author

A:ndrea entered the fields of energy medicine and structural re-alignment in the mid 1990s. Since that time, she has worked to help people clear pain and re-establish greater equilibrium in their lives. Completing studies from Monash at Queensland University of Technology, an ethics and human rights major influenced her post-graduate work.

Within her consultation and teaching roles, she draws upon this background as well as studies in astrology, numerology and Rāja yoga.

Peace here on earth is built from people re-connecting with their own unique senses of purpose and peace. In this transition time from material crisis to spiritual re-emergence, A:ndrea trusts that you will, from now, begin focussing more upon what unites and connects you to other people and this world. She sends to you a prayer: live long – with joy – and flourish.

w: y-om.com

About the Illustrator

Harper is a Melbourne-based tattoo artist with a minimalist, modern and clean art style. Born in the United Kingdom, Harper is a huge believer in manifesting and the power of the Universe. She has faith that the Universe gives us signs when we are on the right path and guides us when we are not.

Harper holds a Bachelor of Arts (honours) at one of the highest ranked universities in the UK. Throughout her teens, Harper explored many different mediums of art until she discovered her passion for handpoke tattoos at the age of 21.

Since then, Harper has taught herself how to tattoo professionally, securing her first studio job just nine months after starting. Harper tattooed for three years in London before emigrating to Australia, where she now works at one of the best tattoo studios in Melbourne.

Harper's work is romantic and feminine, exploring the concepts of love, emotions and inner growth. It is important to Harper that her artwork is created with intention and purpose and that she is connected to what she puts down on paper. She hopes that her artwork will invoke the same inner reflection for the viewer, too.

I: @harperrosetattoo